MW01069433

# BOAT COOKING
## AND ENTERTAINING

# BOAT COOKING

AND ENTERTAINING

Bob Johndrow

641.5753
J65

MCP Books
2301 Lucien Way #415
Maitland, FL 32751
407.339.4217
www.millcitypress.net

© 2019 by Bob Johndrow

All rights reserved. No part of this publication may be reproduced, stored in a retrieval system, or transmitted, in any form or by any means, electronic, mechanical, photocopying, recording, or otherwise, without the prior written permission of the author.

Printed in the United States of America

ISBN-13: 978-1-5456-6725-5

LCCN: 2019940960

# INTRODUCTION

Each weekend during boating season, we invite friends to the marina for dinner and a slow cruise down the river. We start with cocktails and often a simple cheese platter with fresh fruit. We usually take about a two hour cruise up and down the river then return to the harbor where we prepare dinner for our guests. Typically, around sunset we are still drinking wine and settling in with dessert. Sometimes I play the fiddle, and our guests or curious neighbors wander over with other instruments, then we play music on the dock while the moon provides the necessary light for our impromptu jam sessions. Our intent is always to make everyone feel welcome and to have a memorable time while with us on the river. I think we do that well and hope you will get some inspiration to do the same whether cooking on a boat or in another tiny kitchen.

When I told people I was writing a cookbook for people with boats, I had mixed reactions. Some people told me that our boat neighbors only did simple meals such as grilled hot dogs or sandwiches, or that the men mostly cooked and they only wanted to know about barbecue. Others said that they could not really cook anything impressive on a boat due to lack of storage space, limited equipment, or that some boats were too small to have many guests on board. A few encouraging friends told me that they were fascinated by the meals we've served on the boat and wanted to know more about how we managed to make it look so easy. For that reason, I have included my favorite recipes here.

I have always thought food tastes better on the water. Whether you prefer a cabin on a small lake or a cruiser on the water, there is no better place than on a boat to indulge in a cold beverage or glass of wine and enjoy a delicious meal with friends. There's nothing quite as enjoyable as eating on board, but nothing quite as tricky as preparing a delicious feast in a small space with limited tools, ingredients, and often no fridge or oven.

This book is for people who like to cook and entertain with style in a small space. Whether you are cooking on a boat with a tiny galley or any tiny kitchen, this book is for you. The recipes are healthy, using mostly fresh ingredients, lean proteins, healthy fats, whole grains, fresh fruit, and vegetables. Most recipes contain only a few ingredients that mostly come from an organized, well stocked pantry, along with a few fresh ingredients we pick up on our way to the boat.

SPECIAL THANKS TO OUR FRIENDS AND NEIGHBORS AT
WATERGATE MARINA
and
ST. PAUL YACHT CLUB

# TIPS

I have been eating great food for as long as I can remember and cooking for most of my life now. This is our fourth summer cooking for ourselves and others on a boat and we have learned a few tricks that make cooking in a small space possible. The secret to cooking on board is to prepare meals using minimal fresh ingredients and simple techniques that yield maximum flavor. Space is at a premium, so choose your tools carefully.

❖ Things you bring on board should have more than one purpose - a set of measuring cups is essential for measuring, but they may also be used as ladles. On a telescoping boat hook, the hook pops off and becomes a mop or scrub brush. A vegetable peeler doubles as a cheese slicer.

❖ Skip the canned goods - We don't stock canned goods because of space, though most lack flavor and typically have little nutritional value.

❖ Keep a master list of everything you keep on board.

❖ If you're missing an ingredient, be brave and substitute another.

❖ Get a good knife, keep it sharp and store it safely.

❖ Limit kitchen tools and essentials to what is needed for a weekend. Store things such as rice cookers, blenders, pressure cookers off shore and bring on board as needed.

❖ Stock a pantry from the pantry list included here.

❖ Stock a bar with wine, a few spirits, and mixers that will have many uses.

❖ Keep plenty of water on board.

❖ Use serving platters, utensils, dishes, pitchers, martini shakers that are vintage or antique for beautiful presentations.

# PANTRY

- ❖ Salt and pepper
- ❖ Mrs. Dash or Spike (salt substitutes)
- ❖ Thyme
- ❖ Basil
- ❖ Rosemary
- ❖ Oregano
- ❖ Smoked paprika
- ❖ Sesame seeds
- ❖ Onions
- ❖ Garlic
- ❖ Lemons
- ❖ Limes
- ❖ Olive oil
- ❖ Chicken or vegetable stock
- ❖ Canned tomatoes
- ❖ Tomato sauce
- ❖ Vegetable oil
- ❖ Cooking spray
- ❖ Butter
- ❖ Vinegar
- ❖ Mayonnaise
- ❖ Yellow mustard
- ❖ Whole grain mustard
- ❖ Honey
- ❖ Maple syrup
- ❖ Brown sugar
- ❖ Worcestershire
- ❖ Red wine
- ❖ White wine
- ❖ Cognac
- ❖ Vodka
- ❖ Rum
- ❖ Carbonated water
- ❖ Potable water

# TOOLS

- ❖ Nesting pots and pans
- ❖ Cast iron skillet
- ❖ Hot pads or skillet handle pads
- ❖ Whisk
- ❖ Chef's knife and paring knife
- ❖ Cutting board
- ❖ Measuring cups
- ❖ Measuring spoons
- ❖ Spatula
- ❖ Wooden spoons
- ❖ Tongs
- ❖ Spatula
- ❖ Citrus zester
- ❖ Small juicer
- ❖ Small food processor or cup blender
- ❖ Metal skewers
- ❖ Plates
- ❖ Glasses
- ❖ Utensils
- ❖ Aluminum foil
- ❖ Storage bags
- ❖ Plastic garbage bags
- ❖ Paper towels
- ❖ Headlamp for cooking in the dark
- ❖ Corkscrew
- ❖ Can opener
- ❖ Bottle opener
- ❖ Garlic press

# TABLE OF CONTENTS

# COCKTAILS

I assume you and I are similar in many ways. I have always enjoyed having guests over and making them feel special. Creating memorable events involves setting the mood for an environment that is peaceful and comfortable so others feel at ease. Just as in cooking, I use trusted, simple recipes for cocktails over and over. This way I can take care of business without the stress and still take care of guests in a graceful manner.

Nothing on the boat garners more attention than cocktails being mixed in vintage silver plated martini shakers and strained into coupe or martini glasses. The colorful cocktails served in elegant glassware make a lasting impression and are an instant hit. Sliced fresh citrus or fresh herbs create a useful garnish that adds one more layer of flavor to finish off the drink.

I find that I only need to stock a bar with vodka, rum, and wine along with select mixers for a specialty cocktail of the evening. This satisfies most of our visitors, who often bring additional wine as a host gift; there is almost never a shortage of spirits on the boat. Fledgling mixologists assume that the art of craft cocktails needs to be complicated. Traditional recipes are actually not that difficult and following these simple recipes will ensure a perfectly beautiful and refreshing beverage.

When we entertain, we always begin with a few rounds of cocktails to get the evening off to a good start. Cheers!

# MISSISSIPPI BEE STING

The Mississippi Bee Sting is a variation of a Bee's Knees cocktail. Our sting comes from a dose of Ancho de Reyes ancho chile liqueur, since this is the way I was first introduced to this drink on the river. If you go out searching for it, check the tequila section. This liqueur is not tequila but that's typically where you'll find it. I love the way it smells with hints of chile, cinnamon and chocolate.

SERVINGS: 1

**INGREDIENTS:**

2 ounces vodka

1 ounce fresh lemon juice

1 ounce honey-simple syrup

½ ounce Ancho de Reyes liqueur

**METHOD:**

Make honey-simple syrup in advance and chill.

Combine one cup water and one cup honey in a small saucepan.

Heat over medium heat until honey dissolves, stirring occasionally.

When the honey has dissolved, remove from heat and let cool before using.

Simple syrup can be made in advance and stored in a cooler for about three days.

To chill a coupe or martini glass, fill to the top with ice and water.

In a shaker, combine all ingredients listed with ice and shake vigorously.

Empty the glass full of ice, then strain mixture into the chilled glass.

# CRANBERRY VODKA MARTINI

Want to serve a cocktail that is refreshing and something different from the routine boat drinks found around the marina? Then try a simple, cranberry vodka martini. This simple concoction of vodka, cranberry juice, and fresh lime is a perfect cocktail to get the evening started.

SERVINGS: 1

**INGREDIENTS:**

3 ½ ounces vodka

1 ounce cranberry juice

1 ounce fresh squeezed orange

1 lime slice (to garnish)

**METHOD:**

To chill a coupe or martini glass, fill to the top with ice and water.

In a shaker, combine all ingredients listed with ice and shake vigorously.

Empty the glass full of ice, then strain mixture into the chilled glass.

Garnish with lime.

# MOSCOW MULE

Sunny, warm days on the boat with friends pair perfectly with the Moscow Mule. Chilled with a spicy snap of ginger, it's also one that's extremely simple and remains chilled in the copper mug.

Regardless of the name and main ingredients, the Moscow Mule does not come from Russia. It is an American cocktail, cooked up in Manhattan by three men in the beverage industry: one a distributor, one a maker of ginger beer, and one a maker of vodka. They wondered what it would taste like to add two shots of vodka to ginger beer and a squeeze of lime. It worked.

SERVINGS: 1

**INGREDIENTS:**

3 ounces vodka

1 ounce ginger beer

1 lime, quartered

1 bunch mint leaves

**METHOD:**

In a copper mule or glass with ice, combine vodka, juice of one lime, and several torn mint leaves.

Stir, then top it off with ginger beer.

Garnish with a sprig of fresh mint and a lime wedges.

# RUM RUNNER

I was introduced to this drink when I lived in Florida many years ago. As the story goes, Rum Runners were invented in the late 1950s at the Holiday Isle Tiki Bar in Islamorada, Florida. Supposedly, the bar had an excess of rum and certain liqueurs that needed to be moved before the arrival of more inventory. A very tasty concoction was developed using the excess alcohol and the Rum Runner was born. They named the drink after the real "Rum Runners" that inhabited the Florida Keys in the early days.

SERVINGS: 1

**INGREDIENTS:**

4 ounces pineapple juice

4 ounces fresh squeezed orange

1 ounce blackberry liqueur

2 ounces dark rum or aged rum

**METHOD:**

In a martini shaker or small glass pitcher fill with two cups of ice, pineapple juice, orange juice, blackberry liqueur, dark rum and stir.

Pour all ingredients into a tall glass.

# PIÑA COLADA

Everyone has heard of the Piña Colada. It is that delicious, tempting rum, pineapple and coconut cocktail. This is one of the most popular tropical cocktails and this fresh recipe makes a wonderful drink and it is actually very easy. All you need are a few common ingredients, a blender, and some ice.

SERVINGS: 1

**INGREDIENTS:**

2 ounces coconut cream

2 ounces dark rum or aged rum

4 ounces pineapple juice

1 cup ice

**METHOD:**

Add all ingredients to blender.

Make sure the liquids fill the blender to the same level as the ice.

Blend until smooth and creamy.

Pour into a glass.

Garnish with pineapple, lime, and cherry.

# CUBA LIBRE

Commonly known in the United States as a Rum & Coke, the Cuba Libre was invented in Havana around 1900. A simple highball comprised of rum - traditionally Cuban – with cola and lime as a garnish squeezed into the drink. At the end of Batista's rule in Cuba, when Castro took control of the country, there were many celebrations. The drink that welcomed Castro and celebrated "free Cuba" in the late fifties, was the Cuba Libre.

SERVINGS: 2

**INGREDIENTS:**

1 lime, halved

3 ounces dark rum or aged rum

1 bottle sugar cane cola

2 lime slices for garnish

**METHOD:**

Squeeze the juice of half a lime in each of two tall glasses.

Fill the glasses with ice cubes.

Add rum and cola, then stir.

Garnish with lime slices.

# OLD GLORY

Looking for the perfect cocktail for July 4th or any summer weekend? This drink is delightful with bright, colorful muddled berries and a layer of red wine floating on top.

SERVINGS: 1

**INGREDIENTS:**

12 blueberries

2 oz vodka

1 ounce fresh lemon juice

1 ounce simple syrup

2 ounces red wine

**METHOD:**

Make honey-simple syrup in advance and chill.

Combine one cup water and one cup of honey in a small saucepan.

Heat over medium heat until honey dissolves, stirring occasionally.

When the honey has dissolved, remove from heat and let cool before using.

Simple syrup can be made in advance and stored in a cooler for about three days.

Muddle fresh blueberries at the bottom of a double old-fashioned glass and top with ice.

Add vodka, lemon, and simple syrup to a mixing glass and shake vigorously until chilled and combined.

Strain over ice and blueberries.

Carefully pour wine over the back of a spoon into the cocktail to create a layer of red wine floating on top.

# BREAKFAST ON THE BOAT

Mornings are extra special on the boat. We wake up to a light swaying of the boat, feel the fresh cool breeze off the water, yawn, stretch and come to life. First thing in the morning, we're hungry. Depending on the day's plan we could get away with some fresh fruit, yogurt, a breakfast bar, some coffee or hot tea and be on our way. However, we're boating. We enjoy this time of day. So, we have a relaxing, leisurely breakfast on board before embarking on our day's adventures. Here are a few of our favorite, simple breakfast ideas.

# YOGURT PARFAIT

A yogurt parfait is an easy breakfast made by layering yogurt with fresh berries and granola with a drizzle of sweet honey. It's fast, healthy, and easy which makes it the perfect breakfast to serve on a boat. You can use regular yogurt or Greek yogurt depending on your preference.

One of my favorite things about a parfait is that it has a lot of really colorful layers, so I recommend serving this in a clear glass for presentation. If I'm serving this to guests, I might also garnish parfaits with mint leaves and a sprinkle of cinnamon.

SERVINGS: 4

**INGREDIENTS:**

4 cups vanilla yogurt

1 pint fresh raspberries or blueberries

1 cup good quality granola

4 tablespoons honey

**METHOD:**

Fill bottom of a glass with yogurt and press firmly to create a flat surface.

Fill with granola and berries, then another layer of yogurt.

Top with granola and honey and serve immediately.

# RED FLANNEL HASH

I make this from leftovers in a seasoned cast iron skillet. While grilling the night before, I throw a few extra beets and potatoes on the grill and cook both for about an hour and save them for breakfast. The dish is named for the bright red color of the beets, and it has been one of our traditions for many years. This has since become one of our favorite breakfast dishes on the boat.

SERVINGS: 2 - 4

**INGREDIENTS:**

2 tablespoons olive oil

2 tablespoons butter

1 red onion chopped

2 teaspoons minced garlic

2 large beets, cooked, peeled, diced

3 medium potatoes, cooked, peeled, diced

1 teaspoon Worcestershire

1/4 cup fresh basil, chopped

Salt and pepper

**METHOD:**

In a large cast iron skillet, heat the olive oil over high heat, then add butter.

Add the onions and cook until transparent.

Add minced garlic, beets, potatoes and cook stirring occasionally until brown and crisp, about 15 minutes.

If you decide to add eggs, make wells with the back of a spoon and crack a few eggs right on top, then cover and cook about eight more minutes.

Serve in the cast iron skillet but wrap handle with a handle cover or towel.

Top with sour cream if desired.

# SHRIMP AND GRITS

Shrimp and grits are a Southern dish everyone should enjoy. We use shrimp and bacon most of the time, but occasionally substitute the meat for vegetarian hash that might include diced squash, sweet potatoes, beets, or any vegetables left from dinner the night before.

SERVINGS: 6

**INGREDIENTS:**

4 cups water

1 cup stone ground white grits (not instant)

4 tablespoons butter

1 cup shredded cheddar

freshly ground black pepper

6 slices bacon

2 cups cherry tomatoes, halved

1 cup tomato sauce

1 pound large shrimp, peeled and deveined

1 teaspoon dried oregano

1/4 teaspoon paprika

salt and pepper

**METHOD:**

In a medium saucepan, bring 4 cups water to a boil and season with salt. Gradually whisk in grits.

Reduce heat to low and simmer about 45 minutes, adding a little water as needed.

When finished stir in butter and cheese and cover.

Meanwhile, in a large skillet over medium heat, cook bacon and until crispy, about 8 minutes. Leave about 2 tablespoons bacon fat in skillet and drain meat on a paper towel-lined plate. Chop bacon.

Season shrimp with oregano and paprika then add shrimp, cherry tomatoes and tomato sauce to skillet. Cook, stirring occasionally, until shrimp is pink and cooked through, about 4 minutes.

Place tomato sauce in the bottom of each bowl. Top with grits, then shrimp and chopped bacon. Serve with grilled sourdough bread or baguette.

# SHAKSHUKA

Shakshuka, meaning "all mixed up" in Hebrew, is so simple. Eggs are poached in a perfectly spiced vegetarian stew of tomatoes and green peppers. Serve it for breakfast or add a salad and your favorite bread, and you can call it dinner.

SERVINGS: 6 - 8

**INGREDIENTS:**

olive oil

1 large yellow onion, chopped

2 green bell peppers, chopped

2 garlic cloves, peeled, chopped

1 teaspoon ground oregano

1 teaspoon smoked paprika

1/2 teaspoon ground cumin

pinch red pepper flakes

salt and pepper

6 fresh tomatoes, chopped or 28 oz. can strained tomatoes

1/2 cup tomato sauce

1 teaspoon sugar

6 large eggs

1/4 cup chopped fresh parsley leaves

1/4 cup chopped fresh mint leaves

**METHOD:**

In a large cast iron skillet, heat 3 tablespoons olive oil over medium heat.

Add onions, green peppers, garlic, spices, pinch salt and pepper. Cook, stirring frequently, until the vegetables have softened, about ten minutes.

Add the tomatoes, tomato sauce, and sugar. Simmer until the tomato mixture begins to reduce, about twenty minutes.

Make six wells in the tomato mixture with the back of a spoon.

Crack an egg into each indention.

Reduce the heat, cover the skillet, and cook about eight more minutes or until egg whites are set.

Sprinkle parsley and mint leaves over the top and serve.

# HUEVOS RANCHEROS

There are so many variations of huevos rancheros, but this is our version. When the grill is going, I like to toss a few ripe tomatoes in olive oil and grill until a dark char develops and tomatoes become soft. I reserve these tomatoes for bloody Mary mix or salsa. With just a quick pulse in our small mixer, fire roasted tomatoes become ranchero sauce.

SERVINGS: 4

**INGREDIENTS:**

4 fire roasted tomatoes (whole tomatoes tossed in olive oil and grilled until charred)

½ large yellow onion

1 jalapeno, chopped

2 garlic cloves, peeled, chopped

salt and pepper

chipotle chili powder, adobo sauce, or ground cumin to taste (optional)

4 corn tortillas
butter

8 fresh eggs

2 avocados, sliced

2 tablespoons fresh cilantro, chopped (optional)

**METHOD:**

Chop or pulse the fire roasted tomatoes.

In a large skillet, sauté the onions in olive oil over medium heat. Once the onions are translucent, add the tomatoes, garlic and jalapeno.

Add additional chili powder, salt and pepper to taste.

Simmer for ten minutes then reduce heat to low.

In another skillet, heat a teaspoon of olive oil in a large non-stick skillet on medium high, coating the pan with the oil.

Heat the tortillas in the skillet for a minute or two on each side.

Stack warmed tortillas on a plate covered with a towel.

In the skillet used for the tortillas, heat a little butter in the pan over medium heat.

Crack four eggs into the skillet and cook for 3 to 4 minutes for runny yolks, more for firmer eggs.

Transfer the eggs to a plate and cook the remaining four eggs and add salt and pepper to eggs as desired.

To serve, place a few avocado slices on a tortilla, topped with eggs and ranchero sauce.

Garnish with fresh cilantro.

# APPETIZERS

We sometimes make a meal of appetizers or small plates, so these are not necessarily a first course in all cases. Simple preparation and great flavor make these appetizers work for many different needs. Start the party with these or make a meal for your guests that they are sure to enjoy.

# CATALAN TOMATO BREAD

On our first trip to Spain, we tried many different versions of this and they were all incredible. Our favorite, however, is this recipe that involves rubbing raw garlic on grilled bread, then topping it with fresh grated tomatoes, olive oil and salt. You can assemble it for your guests or provide them with ingredients and allow them to build their own.

SERVINGS: 6 - 8

**INGREDIENTS:**

4 ripe tomatoes

extra virgin olive oil

1 clove garlic

sea salt

1 artisan bread boule such as sourdough

**METHOD:**

Slice the bread into half inch slices, then cut each slice in fourths.

Brush bread with olive oil and grill over medium heat for a few minutes on each side, then remove from grill.

Wash and dry the tomatoes.

Cut the tomatoes in half and grate them using a box grater, discarding the stem and skins.

Cut the clove of garlic in half and rub the raw garlic on the toasted bread.

Spoon the tomato pulp over the toast, then drizzle the extra virgin olive oil and add a sprinkle of sea salt.

# MEDITERRANEAN SHRIMP SKEWERS

We enjoy having seafood on the boat, especially this simple method in which the shrimp are seasoned very simply with oregano, sweet paprika, and a garlic paste with an olive oil and citrus marinade. Marinate the shrimp for at least a few hours to allow it to absorb all the flavors of the marinade.

We skewer them and cook them on the grill quickly over high heat. When the shrimp skewers are ready, they will turn pink; if you leave the tail on, it will turn bright red. The shrimp should be firm and served hot.

SERVINGS: 8

**INGREDIENTS:**

2 pounds large shrimp peeled, deveined, tail-on

8 garlic cloves

1 tablespoon dried oregano

1 teaspoon smoked paprika

extra virgin olive oil

2 lemons juiced

**METHOD:**

Clean the shrimp and place in a mixing bowl.

Smash the garlic clove with the back of a knife, then mince the garlic.

Add the garlic, oregano, and smoke paprika. Add a cup of olive oil, fresh lemon juice and toss everything with the shrimp.

Marinate in a covered bowl for a few hours.

Thread shrimp on metal skewers.

Brush the grill with olive oil using a paper towel.

Grill the skewered shrimp for about four minutes per side.

Line a platter with mixed greens or micro greens and place skewers on top.

Offer lemon wedges to squeeze over the top if desired.

# SHRIMP COCKTAIL

We often serve shrimp cocktail on the boat. Source the best fresh seafood you can find and create your own cocktail sauce. This is one of our favorites, as it is flavorful and easy. For a beautiful presentation, find a large martini glass to hold the cocktail sauce. Hang the shrimp from the rim and add sliced lemons.

SERVINGS: 4

**INGREDIENTS:**

24 large shrimp

1 bottle white wine

1 tablespoon Old Bay seasoning

1 cup ketchup

2 tablespoons horseradish

1 lemon, juiced

1 tablespoon Worcestershire

1 teaspoon hot sauce

1 lemon, sliced

**METHOD:**

Fill a large saucepan with bottle of wine and water to fill the pan.

Add Old Bay seasoning and lemon juice.

Bring the pot to a rapid boil over high heat.

Remove from the heat and let it stop boiling.

Add the shrimp. Put a lid on the saucepan. Let sit for five minutes, until shrimp are opaque and pink.

Meanwhile, prepare a bowl with ice water.

When shrimp are cooked, spoon shrimp into the bowl of ice water.

Peel and devein shrimp but leave the tails on.

In a mixing bowl combine the ketchup, horseradish, lemon juice, Worcestershire sauce and hot sauce.

Taste, then add more horseradish if desired.

Divide sauce among four martini glasses.

Hang shrimp from the rim.

Garnish each glass with sliced lemon wedges.

# GRILLED CHEESE AND JALAPEÑO QUESADILLAS

This is a simple appetizer that can be cooked in a skillet or directly on the grill, depending on whatever seems to be most easily accessible. They can be served hot or room temperature if you wish. Be sure to remove the seeds from the jalapeños to ensure less heat. I usually do about half without the jalapeños.

SERVINGS: 8

**INGREDIENTS:**

16 corn tortillas

vegetable oil

8 ounces spreadable cream cheese

smoked paprika, chile powder

6 bacon strips, cooked and chopped

4 jalapeno peppers, seeded and finely chopped

1 cup shredded sharp cheddar cheese

1 cup shredded mozzarella

**METHOD:**

Arrange 8 tortillas on a clean surface.

With a rubber spatula, spread cream cheese on each tortilla.

Layer with jalapeños, then cheese.

Top with remaining tortillas.

Heat a cast iron grill pan or skillet over medium heat with a little vegetable oil.

Cook quesadillas cheese side down for two to three minutes, then flip and cook the other side for another two to three minutes. Press down with a weighted panini press or another heavy skillet while cooking.

Cut in fourths and serve warm.

# GOAT CHEESE STUFFED DATES WITH CURED BACON

These make an amazing appetizer with just a few ingredients. They are perfect for any kind of party or gathering. Our bacon wrapped dates are now legendary and made with real pitted dates, tangy goat cheese, and a crisp outer layer of bacon. For these, I use a cast iron skillet in the galley or the same skillet over a hot grill.

SERVINGS: 8

**INGREDIENTS:**

20 whole pitted dates

3 ounces goat cheese

10 strips of smoked bacon
honey

Worcestershire

**METHOD:**

If dates are not pitted, carefully cut along one side and remove the pit without cutting the date in half.

Spread open each date and stuff with a small teaspoon of goat cheese, scraping the cheese off the tip of the spoon into the date.

Sprinkle with fresh thyme, a drop of honey, and a few drops of Worcestershire sauce.

Cut each strip of bacon in half

Roll each date inside of the bacon, making sure to seal the opening well.

Seal with a toothpick.

Heat a cast iron skillet over medium heat.

Cook one side of each bacon wrapped date until browned, about four minutes, then turn and cook the other side about four more minutes. Covering the pan will ensure more even cooking and avoid grease from splattering.

Remove from pan, drain on paper towels and serve warm or at room temperature.

# SESAME SALMON BITES WITH ROASTED RED PEPPER

Salmon bites provide a healthy seafood option to your event. Simply pressed in sesame seeds and sautéed for a few minutes on each side, they are such a nice touch.

SERVINGS: 8

**INGREDIENTS:**

1 cup sesame seeds

2 tablespoons yellow mustard

4 4-ounce salmon fillets, cut into one-inch segments

vegetable oil

1 jar roasted red peppers

1 baguette

Salt and pepper

**METHOD:**

Place sesame seeds in a shallow bowl. Rub salmon fillets with mustard and sprinkle with salt and pepper. Press flesh side of fillets in sesame seeds to coat.

Warm remaining vegetable oil in a large nonstick skillet over high heat about two to three minutes.

Place salmon fillets, skin side down, in skillet; reduce heat to medium-high and cook until skin is browned, and bottom halves of fillets are opaque, about four minutes.

Turn and cook until fish is done, about three minutes for medium-rare.

Transfer to a platter, flipping fillets so seed side is up.

Slice baguette into thin slices.

Serve salmon atop baguette slices and garnish with roasted red peppers.

# PROSCIUTTO WRAPPED ASPARAGUS

I start with home-made refrigerator asparagus pickles as they have a much lighter flavor than canned asparagus pickles. They are ready to eat in just a few days, but if you can manage to wait a week they will be even better. The pickled asparagus is simply dressed in a little cream cheese and wrapped with prosciutto.

SERVINGS: 8

**INGREDIENTS:**

2 pounds fresh asparagus spears, cleaned and trimmed

1 pint water

½ cup apple cider vinegar

1 tablespoon kosher salt

1 tablespoons sugar

4 cloves garlic, smashed

1 bunch fresh dill

1 teaspoon whole mustard seeds

1 lemon, sliced

8 ounces spreadable cream cheese

12 ounces prosciutto

**METHOD:**

In a large stock pot, bring water to a boil.

Prepare a large bowl of ice water.

When water comes to a boil, add asparagus spears and boil for 15 seconds.

Remove asparagus and transfer it to the bowl of ice water.

Bring the pint of water, vinegar, salt, and sugar to a boil, stirring to dissolve the salt and sugar.

Let the brine cool slightly while you load the jars.

Place sliced lemon and garlic cloves in the jars.

Place the jar on its side and start loading in the asparagus spears, adding the dill, and mustard seeds.

Pour the cooled brine into the jar over the other ingredients.

Once the asparagus has marinated for at least two days, remove what you will be using and pat dry with a paper towel.

With a butter knife, smear a little cream cheese on the center of the asparagus.

Wrap a half slice of prosciutto around each asparagus spear and arrange on a platter.

# DINNER FOR SMALL GROUPS

We take dinner seriously, whether it is a casual dinner for two or a more elegant dinner for a small group of friends. The table is a gathering place for sharing food and making memories. Things that can be mostly prepared in advance or made to order in a simple manner allow us to spend more time together lingering over a great meal. Simple cooking techniques and fresh ingredients make all the difference.

The recipes here rely heavily on ingredients from a stocked pantry, along with a few fresh ingredients from the market. I have been cooking many of these for years and they are among our favorites when having guests on the boat for dinner.

# BISON SLIDERS WITH GORGONZOLA CREAM

These savory bacon sliders use lean bison topped with bacon, avocado and a delicious gorgonzola cream to create a beautiful platter to pass amongst your guests. We serve them on toasted sesame buns or dollar rolls.

SERVINGS: 4

**INGREDIENTS:**

2 cups whipping cream

4 ounces gorgonzola crumbles

4 ounces Parmesan

1 pound ground buffalo meat

4 cloves garlic, minced

3 tablespoons Worcestershire

salt and pepper

leaf lettuce

1 avocado, cleaned and sliced

6 strips bacon cooked, cut in thirds

8 small sesame buns or dollar rolls

**METHOD:**

In a small sauce pan, heat cream to boiling and reduce by half.

Remove cream from heat, then whisk in gorgonzola and parmesan and set aside.

Combine the buffalo meat, garlic, Worcestershire, salt and pepper in a mixing bowl. Mix with hands by blending everything together.

Form meat into eight golf ball sized balls, then press into small patties.

Grill patties over medium high heat for about three minutes per side and remove from grill.

To toast buns, place buns on hot grill for about one minute.

Place bottom half of buns on platter.

Add leaf lettuce, burger, avocado, and a few pieces of bacon to cover each.

Drizzle cheese sauce over each and top with bun.

Serve warm.

# LOW COUNTRY SHRIMP BOIL

Our shrimp boil is made with a combination of shrimp, sausage, corn and potatoes. It's a perfect dish to create to please a crowd. Though traditionally all ingredients are boiled or steamed in a large pot, we toss everything together and wrap it in foil with butter, then let everything steam together over the grill. We keep the same outdoor component but eliminate the stockpot in favor of easy foil packets.

SERVINGS: 4

**INGREDIENTS:**

1 pound large fresh shrimp, peeled and deveined

6 ounces fully cooked andouille sausage

1 pound baby red potatoes, diced small

2 ears corn the cob, husked and cut into two-inch pieces

4 tablespoons butter

4 tablespoons vegetable oil

2 tablespoons seafood seasoning

1 lemon, quartered

chopped fresh parsley

**METHOD:**

In a large bowl, place the shrimp, sausage, potatoes, and corn.

Add the melted butter with vegetable oil, and seafood seasoning.

Toss to combine.

Preheat an outdoor grill to medium high heat.

Place four large pieces of aluminum foil on the counter.

Mound the shrimp and sausage mixture in the center of each piece, dividing it evenly between the four, with one quartered lemon in each packet.

Bring the shorter edges to the center, then fold them over each other to make a seam in the center.

Fold in the edges to seal so that you create a packet. Leave some space inside of each packet for air to circulate.

Place packets on the grill and cover.

Grill for 10 minutes on the first side, then flip and continue grilling for 5 additional minutes until the shrimp are cooked through and the vegetables are tender.

Carefully open the foil packets.

Remove the corn and grill for a few minutes on each side to add a little char to each piece.

Serve hot on individual plates with a sprinkle of chopped parsley.

# BEEF DAUBE

This beef simmers all day in red wine. A classic French braised beef, red wine, and vegetable stew is simple and delicious. It stands above so many other beef recipes because it offers the homey comfort and convenience of a pot roast, yet is simple and sophisticated enough for entertaining. We use an induction burner and shore power for this recipe.

SERVINGS: 8

**INGREDIENTS:**

2 teaspoons olive oil

1 boneless beef chuck roast about 2 pounds cut into 1-inch cubes

salt and pepper

2 cups rough cut carrots

1/2 yellow onion, chopped

12 garlic cloves, crushed and minced

1 tablespoon tomato paste

1 bottle red wine

1 can diced tomatoes

1/2 cup beef broth

1 teaspoon chopped fresh rosemary

1 teaspoon chopped fresh thyme

1 bay leaf

1 teaspoon ground cloves

hot cooked pasta or mashed potatoes

fresh thyme for garnish

**METHOD:**

In a large skillet, heat oil over medium heat.

Season meat with salt and pepper.

Brown meat in small batches.

Transfer beef to a Dutch oven.

Add carrot, onions, garlic and salt and pepper to skillet, then cook and stir until golden brown, about six minutes.

Add tomato paste and cook and stir until fragrant, about one minute.

Add red wine, stirring to loosen browned bits from pan and reduce liquid by half.

Add red wine, tomatoes, broth and herbs to Dutch oven with the beef.

Cook, covered, on low heat until tender, about six to seven hours.

Discard bay leaf.

Serve over hot cooked pasta or mashed potatoes.

If desired, garnish with fresh thyme.

# LAMB CHOPS WITH BERRY GASTRIQUE

We use freshly picked raspberries to make this Berry Gastrique and serve it with lamb chops and greens, but you can substitute other berries. Blueberries or wild blackberries also make a fabulous gastrique for lamb. A gastrique is a reduction of vinegar and sugar that is simple, flavorful, and makes a beautiful presentation.

SERVINGS: 2

**INGREDIENTS:**

4 lamb chops

vegetable oil

salt and pepper

1 teaspoon salt

1 cup sugar

4 tablespoons water

1/4 cup white wine vinegar

¼ cup white wine

2 cups fresh berries

2 sprigs fresh thyme

**METHOD:**

Season the lamb chops with salt and pepper and set aside.

To make the gastrique, combine sugar and water in a small saucepan.

Stir until completely dissolved and bubbles form.

When it turns a light caramel color, add the vinegar all at once.

The sugar will harden immediately, and the mixture will appear flaky.

Continue to cook and stir, until the mixture becomes liquid again.

Add the wine and cook until it is reduced and syrupy.

Add the berries and thyme and stir to incorporate.

Remove from heat.

Heat a skillet over medium heat and add vegetable oil.

Place lamb chops in skillet for about five minutes, then carefully flip.

Cook on the other side for about four minutes for medium rare.

Serve lamb over greens drizzled with gastrique.

# TORTILLA ESPAÑOLA

I first tried this in Spain and have been serving it often on the boat since then. Tortilla Española or Spanish omelet is a simple potato recipe dish that can be enjoyed hot or cold, as a starter or a main course. Often it is carried along and served cold at a picnic.

SERVINGS: 4-6

**INGREDIENTS:**

1 pound waxy potatoes

1½ teaspoon salt

2¼ cups olive oil

1 onion

4 eggs

**METHOD:**

Rinse and peel potatoes. Cut them into quarters length-wise then slice thinly.

Pour two cups of oil into a seven-inch skillet.

Turn heat to high and add two cups olive oil.

When the oil is hot, add sliced potatoes and reduce the heat to medium. Fry the potatoes for five minutes, stirring occasionally.

In a mixing bowl beat 4 eggs. Season with a generous pinch of salt.

When the potatoes are cooked, drain the excess oil and add them into the bowl with beaten eggs. Mix everything together and let rest for five minutes.

Heat ¼ cup of olive oil in the skillet. Wait until the oil is hot and then pour in the potato mixture. Push down the edges with a spatula. Let it cook until the edges are set (a few minutes).

Cover the pan with a large plate. With one hand hold the plate tight and with the other one hold the handle of your skillet. Flip over the skillet so that the plate is underneath.

Lift the empty pan/skillet and place it back onto the heat. Add little oil. Slide the omelet back into the pan. Cook until eggs are set.

# CORNFLAKE CRUSTED CHICKEN

I've been making this for many years, but mostly in my home kitchen because we make it in large quantities and bring it to the boat, to dock parties, and to picnics. Everyone can enjoy this gluten free version of crunchy cornflake crusted chicken served hot or cold. This can also be prepared in the galley, using the oven and small baking sheets.

SERVINGS: 4-6

**INGREDIENTS:**

4 boneless, skinless chicken breasts, sliced into long thin strips about 1-inch wide

3 cups corn flakes

2 cups grated Parmesan

2 tablespoons olive oil

1 large egg

1 teaspoon water

3 tablespoons dried basil
salt

pepper

**METHOD:**

Preheat oven to 400 degrees.

Sprinkle salt, pepper and basil on chicken.

Mix egg and water in a bowl.

In another large bowl, crush cornflakes and add parmesan, olive oil and mix.

Dip chicken strips into egg wash and roll in the cornflake crust to coat. Press chicken into cornflake mix with force to ensure a good coating.

Place chicken on oven sheet and sprinkle extra cornflake mix over the top of all the chicken strips.

Bake at 400 for about thirty minutes.

# CHICKEN PICCATA

Impress your guests with this classic Italian American dish that is both savory and a little tart from the sauce of fresh squeezed lemon, finished with white wine, butter, and capers. When you want a delicious, economical, simple meal that takes merely minutes, you can't beat it. While it is often served over buttered pasta, try serving it with steamed spinach, quinoa, or rice.

SERVINGS: 2 - 4

**INGREDIENTS:**

1 pound boneless skinless chicken breasts

salt and pepper

4 tablespoons butter

2 tablespoons olive oil

4 cloves garlic, minced

3 cups white wine

2 cups chicken stock

3 tablespoons honey

1 large lemon, sliced thinly

2 tablespoons butter

¼ cup capers

fresh Italian parsley, chopped

**METHOD:**

Cut each chicken breast in half, then pound the chicken thin by placing between two sheets of film wrap and pounding with a clean cast iron skillet until each breast is uniform in thickness, about ½ inch in thickness.

Heat the oil and butter in a large skillet over medium heat.

Add 2 chicken breasts to the pan and sear until golden brown, about three minutes per side, then remove from skillet.

Add the remaining 2 chicken breasts, sear about three minutes per side, then remove from skillet.

Add garlic and sauté until fragrant, about one minute.

Deglaze the pan by adding wine and scraping bottom of skillet.

Add chicken stock, lemon juice, sliced lemons, honey, and place the chicken back in the pan.

Cook over high heat until liquid has reduced by half.

Turn off the heat, stir in two more tablespoons of butter along with capers.

Return chicken to the pan and coat with sauce.

Add fresh chopped Italian parsley and either serve from the sauté pan, or plate individual dishes with chicken served over buttered pasta if desired.

# PAN SEARED SCALLOPS WITH PEA PESTO

An elegant meal that is simple to prepare. The pea pesto can easily be made in advance and reheated in a skillet, while the seared scallops are the star of this plate for sure. Dry pack scallops should be purchased as fresh as possible and prepared the same day.

SERVINGS: 4

**INGREDIENTS:**

10 ounce bag of frozen peas, defrosted

1 clove garlic, peeled

4 stalks fresh basil, chopped

2 tablespoon fresh lemon juice

1 cup extra virgin olive oil

1 cup grated Parmesan cheese

salt and pepper

1 tablespoon butter

1 tablespoon extra virgin olive oil

12 large sea scallops

**METHOD:**

Place peas, garlic, basil, and lemon juice in the bowl of a Bullet mixer.

Process until well combined. Pour in olive oil and mix until smooth.

Transfer mixture to a medium bowl, then add cheese, salt, and pepper.

Remove tendon from scallops by peeling it away and discarding.

Season scallops with salt and pepper.

Heat a large cast iron skillet over medium high heat.

Add butter and olive oil.

When pan is almost smoking, add scallops, leaving space between each one.

Sear for 1 to 2 minutes on each side or until lightly browned.

Do not overcook.

Transfer to a plate and let rest for 2 to 3 minutes.

Spread a spoonful of pesto on each plate and place three scallops on pesto.

Garnish with pea shoots or micro greens.

# GRILLED PERSIAN CHICKEN KABOBS

This is one of my favorite recipes for entertaining. Ground chicken is seasoned with lemon, garlic and spices, then grilled on skewers until golden brown. Serve with grilled tomatoes and steamed rice.

SERVINGS: 4

**INGREDIENTS:**

6 garlic cloves

1 pound ground chicken breast

1 onion grated

1/4 teaspoon cumin

¼ teaspoon cinnamon

1 tablespoon smoked paprika

salt and pepper

1 lemon, juiced

2 tablespoons vegetable oil

¼ bunch parsley, minced

1 bunch fresh dill, torn

**METHOD:**

Place ground chicken breast in a large bowl.

Finely dice or use garlic press to mince and add garlic to chicken.

Add ground cumin, cinnamon, smoked paprika, lemon, salt and pepper.

Add grated onion into the bowl, with vegetable oil, parsley and mix.

Cover the bowl with plastic wrap and keep it in a refrigerator for at least two hours.

Remove the bowl from the refrigerator.

Form ball of the mixture, then shape into a three-inch log, and press around skewers.

Preheat a grill to high.

Clean and oil the grill, then grill the chicken kabobs until cooked through, turning four times, about two minutes per side.

Garnish with fresh dill.

# PAN SEARED SALMON WITH HONEY-LEMON GLAZE

With a cast iron skillet, this pan seared salmon develops a beautifully caramelized crust while the salmon remains moist and tender with a sweet garlic, honey and lemon glaze. When pan searing salmon, wait until a golden crust forms. If the flesh sticks to the pan, give it a just a little longer, then flip. Try and purchase salmon with the skin on.

SERVINGS: 4

**INGREDIENTS:**

salt and pepper

4 salmon fillets, skin on

2 tablespoons olive oil

1 tablespoon butter

4 garlic cloves minced

4 tablespoons honey

3 tablespoons fresh squeezed lemon juice

chopped parsley

**METHOD:**

Season salmon with salt and pepper.

Add oil then butter to a cast iron skillet over high heat.

When the butter has melted, add salmon to the pan skin side down.

Cook salmon for about 5 minutes, skin side down and adjust heat to medium.

Flip the salmon and cook for another 3 minutes, then turn heat to low.

Add garlic to the pan around the salmon and cook until fragrant.

Add honey and lemon juice to pan and continue cooking everything together.

Salmon is ready when it feels firm to the touch and looks opaque.

Remove salmon and place on serving plates, skin side down.

With a wooden spoon, stir remaining ingredients in the pan, then pour this over each salmon fillet.

Garnish with chopped parsley.

# PORK CHOPS WITH APPLE CIDER SAUCE

Pan seared pork chops are among our favorites. Pork chops are cooked in just a few minutes, then finished with apples and the natural juices that create a delicious apple cider sauce. The pork chops and a fresh salad make a perfect meal.

SERVINGS: 4

**INGREDIENTS:**

4 thick center cut pork chops

2 tablespoons vegetable oil

4 garlic cloves, minced

4 apples, cored and thinly sliced

3 cups unfiltered apple cider

2 cups chicken stock or chicken broth

3 tablespoons apple cider vinegar

3 tablespoons Dijon mustard

2 tablespoons Worcestershire

3 tablespoons butter

salt and pepper

fresh thyme

**METHOD:**

Place pork chops on a plate, pat them dry with a paper towel, then season with salt and pepper.

Heat a large skillet over medium high heat, then add vegetable oil.

When the oil is hot, add the pork chops one at a time, with plenty of space so they are not over crowded.

Sear the pork chops for about three minutes until golden brown, then flip each pork chop and sear the other side.

Remove the pork chops to a plate and cover with foil.

In the same skillet, add a little more oil, garlic, and apples, then sauté until the apples form a golden crust.

Add apple cider, chicken broth, apple cider vinegar, and Dijon mustard.

Bring to a boil, then lower the heat just a little.

Return the pork chops to the pan and cook until braising liquid is reduced by half, about 15 minutes.

When finished, remove pork chops from the pan.

Turn heat to high, then add butter and Worcestershire sauce to the remaining braising liquid. Reduce the sauce a little more to create a glaze that will coat the back of a spoon.

Pour apples and apple cider sauce on a large platter, then place pork chops on top.

Garnish with fresh thyme.

# HARISSA CHICKEN

Harissa is a spicy and aromatic chili paste that's a widely used staple in North African and Middle Eastern cooking. Harissa recipes vary between countries and regions, but a standard version includes a blend of smoked chili peppers, garlic, olive oil and spices, like cumin, coriander, caraway and mint. Tomatoes and rose petals are also common ingredients. It basically brings alive any dish you're making because of its color and aromatic flavor. You can find harissa in a jar or tube in most grocery stores' international foods section. We usually serve it over rice with an arugula and tomato salad.

SERVINGS: 4

**INGREDIENTS:**

4 tablespoons olive oil

4 tablespoons harissa

4 garlic cloves minced

1 tablespoon smoked paprika

1 tablespoon cumin

salt and pepper

2 pounds chicken breast cut into large chunks

4 multi-colored carrots, cooked, sliced thin

1 lemon, juiced

**METHOD:**

In a large bowl, combine olive oil, harissa, garlic, paprika, cumin, salt and pepper. Add the chicken and carrots and mix well.

Refrigerate for a few hours.

Heat a large saucepan, then transfer the chicken from the bowl to the saucepan.

Cook for about ten minutes or until the chicken is well done, then add fresh lemon.

Serve over rice with garnish of lime wedges.

# SALADS

These healthy salad recipes are perfect for anyone looking to add a little more nutrition to their diet. I think a great salad can substitute for a meal, so I have included those that may stand alone, or perhaps pair with a few appetizers for a more complete meal. These are among our favorites; I hope you will enjoy them as well.

# WATERMELON FETA SALAD

Watermelon Feta Salad is just watermelon dressed up and makes such a beautiful presentation. Salty feta plays off the sweetness of the melon, while fresh mint takes it to a whole new level. A dash of lime and Worcestershire gives it just the kick it needs. The sweet and tangy flavors work so well together I wonder why this is not served at every summer get together. Once the melon is diced, the dish is ready within a few minutes.

SERVINGS: 2-4

**INGREDIENTS:**

6 cups cubed watermelon

2 tablespoons lime juice

1 tablespoon Worcestershire

1 bunch fresh mint, chopped

1/2 cup feta, crumbled

fresh cracked pepper

**METHOD:**

Prepare watermelon and dice in small cubes.

Place watermelon in a large bowl.

Drizzle lime juice and Worcestershire over watermelon.

Add mint and most of the feta, and lightly toss.

Transfer to a serving dish.

Add the remaining feta, then add fresh cracked pepper.

# SEAFOOD COBB WITH CITRUS VINAIGRETTE

This is a classic Cobb salad with a light summer twist. A light, filling salad loaded with sautéed shrimp, bacon, avocado, tomatoes and roasted corn in a tangy, refreshing vinaigrette makes a delightful meal on board. The shrimp and vinaigrette can be prepared in advance and stored until needed. Everything can then be tossed together just before serving. Substitute or add steamed and chilled seafood of your choice such as crab or lobster if desired.

SERVINGS: 2

**INGREDIENTS:**

1 pound medium shrimp, peeled and deveined

2 tablespoons olive oil

1 tablespoon smoked paprika

4 slices bacon, cooked and diced

2 hard boiled eggs, diced

5 cups chopped romaine lettuce

1 cup cherry tomatoes

1 avocado diced

2 ears of corn, grilled then shucked

fresh dill for garnish

**FOR THE CITRUS VINAIGRETTE**

1 lime, juiced

1 lemon, juiced

2 cloves garlic, minced

1 tablespoon Worcestershire

1 teaspoon honey

2 tablespoons olive oil

2 tablespoons vinegar

salt and pepper

**METHOD:**
**VINAIGRETTE:**

To make the citrus vinaigrette, combine, lime juice, lemon juice and garlic, Worcestershire, and honey. Whisk all ingredients briskly, then while whisking slowly pour in olive oil until emulsified and then set aside.

**SALAD:**

In a mixing bowl, add shrimp, olive oil and smoked paprika, and gently toss together.

Heat a large skillet over medium high heat.

Add shrimp to pan and sauté for about three minutes, then flip.

Cook the other side for about two minutes or until shrimp are pink and firm.

To assemble the salad, place romaine lettuce in a large bowl; top with arranged rows avocado, eggs, bacon, warm or chilled shrimp, tomatoes, and corn.

Serve immediately with citrus vinaigrette poured over the top of all ingredients.

# CAPRESE WITH BALSAMIC REDUCTION

Our garden is small, but we manage to make room for tomatoes and herbs mostly. Our favorite thing about summer is home grown tomatoes. A ripe, juicy, summer heirloom tomato is so vastly superior to the sad, flavorless supermarket tomatoes you'll find out of season.

All we add to the fresh, ripe tomatoes is a milky mozzarella, fragrant fresh basil, a drizzle of olive oil, a spoonful of balsamic glaze, and sea salt to help draw out the sweet tomato juices.

SERVINGS: 4-6

**INGREDIENTS:**

4 ripe tomatoes, sliced thin

1 pound fresh mozzarella cheese, sliced same thickness as tomatoes

1/2 cup packed fresh basil leaves

sea salt

black pepper

2 tablespoons olive oil

1 cup balsamic vinegar cooked over high heat for about 20 minutes until the vinegar thickens, coats the back of a spoon, and is reduced to about three or four tablespoons, then cooled.

**METHOD:**

On a platter, arrange tomatoes, mozzarella, and basil on a platter in an alternating pattern.

Sprinkle with a generous pinch of sea salt and several grinds of black pepper, to taste.

Drizzle with the olive oil and balsamic reduction

# SPINACH SALAD WITH SALMON, BERRIES AND MUSTARD VINAIGRETTE

The beauty of this spinach salad is the variety of berries used to keep the flavors interesting. The savory mustard vinaigrette pairs well with salmon and elevates the salad. This makes a wonderful dinner for two but could just as easily be served for a large group on a beautiful serving platter.

SERVINGS: 2

## MUSTARD VINAIGRETTE

Makes one cup and can be stored for up to two weeks refrigerated.

### INGREDIENTS:

2 tablespoons orange juice, fresh squeezed

2 tablespoons minced shallots

1 tablespoon dried tarragon

1 tablespoon Dijon mustard

2 tablespoons whole grain mustard

2 tablespoons honey

¼ cup vinegar

½ cup extra virgin olive oil

salt and pepper

### METHOD:

Add the orange juice, shallots, and tarragon to a bowl. Slowly start whisking all ingredients, then add mustards, honey, and vinegar. While whisking briskly, slowly pour in the oil. Season with a little salt and pepper.

## SALMON

### INGREDIENTS:

4 tablespoons vegetable oil

2 tablespoons butter

2 salmon fillets, skin on

salt and pepper

### METHOD:

Pat salmon dry and brush both sides with vegetable oil.

Heat a nonstick frying pan over medium-high heat and cook salmon skin-side down for three minutes, or until edges turn golden.

Flip and cook on other side for two minutes more, until just cooked through.

Season with salt and pepper.

Transfer to a plate.

## SALAD

### INGREDIENTS:

4 cups spinach leaves

1 cup strawberries, cleaned and halved

1 cup blueberries

1 cup blackberries

### METHOD:

Place spinach in a large mixing bowl.

Add berries, then toss with vinaigrette.

Plate spinach salad on each plate, then place salmon on top.

# ROASTED BEETS, GOAT CHEESE AND ARUGULA

Our roasted beet salad is very filling and packed with flavor. We roast the beets on the grill just before dinner. The beets are then served warm and work well with the peppery arugula, goat cheese, and simple vinaigrette.

SERVINGS: 2

**INGREDIENTS:**
**SALAD:**

8 roasted baby beets (unpeeled beets grilled for about 30-40 minutes until fork tender, then peeled and sliced)

2 large handfuls fresh arugula

4 tablespoons goat cheese

**VINAIGRETTE:**

2 tablespoons fresh squeezed lemon juice

2 tablespoons vinegar

1 teaspoon sugar

3 tablespoons olive oil

salt and pepper

**METHOD:**

For vinaigrette, add lemon, vinegar, and sugar to a small mixing bowl.

Whisk all ingredients briskly.

While still whisking, slowly pour in the olive oil.

Add salt and pepper to taste.

Assemble the salads on each plate by placing arugula leaves, sliced beets, and goat cheese

Drizzle the salad with vinaigrette and add fresh cracked pepper.

# SIDES

Side dishes should not be an afterthought. While we tend to give more thought to the pork, beef, seafood, or chicken dishes, we try to plan for side dishes that will accompany things well. Whether you are hosting or attending a dinner, you'll want to have several delicious side dishes that you feel comfortable making and know that pretty much everyone else will love.

# GRILLED ASPARAGUS WITH ROASTED GARLIC AND LEMON

Grilled asparagus is so easy and quick to make. Charred and smoky asparagus are tossed in a roasted garlic, lemon butter and then topped with ample Parmesan cheese. Preparing asparagus on the grill or in a cast iron grill pan is so simple and delicious.

SERVINGS: 2-4

**INGREDIENTS:**

1 pound asparagus, trimmed

2 tablespoons olive oil

salt and pepper

2 tablespoons butter

4 garlic cloves, minced

2 teaspoons fresh squeezed lemon

4 tablespoons Parmesan cheese

2 lemons, halved

**METHOD:**

Heat the grill

In a mixing bowl, toss the asparagus with olive oil, salt and pepper.

In a small sauce pan melt the butter over medium heat, then add the garlic and fresh squeezed lemon. Cook until fragrant, about three minutes, then remove from heat.

Place the asparagus on the grill in a row, or in a grill basket over the heat. Grill for about five minutes over high heat, turning occasionally until they are charred.

Remove the asparagus from the grill and place them on a serving plate. Pour the melted butter, garlic, lemon mixture over the top and toss gently.

Top with grated Parmesan cheese.

Serve immediately.

# SESAME GREEN BEANS

These fresh green beans tossed in an Asian inspired dressing and sprinkled with sesame seeds make a nice accompaniment to many main course dishes.

SERVINGS: 4-6

**INGREDIENTS:**

1 pound French green beans, trimmed

3 tablespoons sesame seeds

6 garlic cloves, minced

1 tablespoon grated ginger

2 tablespoons soy sauce

1 tablespoon Worcestershire

2 tablespoons rice vinegar

2 tablespoons olive oil

**METHOD:**

Toss green beans in a little olive oil and grill for about five minutes.

Meanwhile whisk together garlic, ginger, soy sauce, vinegar, and oil in a large bowl.

When green beans are tender add them to the bowl and toss. Sprinkle with sesame seeds.

Serve hot or cold.

# BLISTERED TOMATOES WITH AVOCADO CREAM

You can make these the perfectionist way, with every tomato blistered yet holding its shape, or you can do my version, where they hang together in a flavorful garlic oil. The blistered tomatoes can be served warm or chilled, along with this delicious avocado cream.

SERVINGS: 4-6

**AVOCADO CREAM**

**INGREDIENTS:**

2 ripe avocados, pitted, peeled, then cut into large pieces

2 limes, juiced

½ cup sour cream

salt

**METHOD:**

Place all ingredients except salt in a mixing bowl.

Mash with a fork, then whisk until all ingredients are incorporated.

Add salt to taste.

**ROASTED TOMATOES**

**INGREDIENTS:**

1 tablespoon olive oil

2 pints grape tomatoes

4 cloves garlic, minced

fresh basil, chopped

**METHOD:**

In a heavy skillet heat the oil over medium-high heat.

Add the tomatoes to the hot pan and cook for about two minutes without stirring, until charred.

Stir the tomatoes, then add the garlic to the pan.

Turn heat to low and continue cooking for another two minutes until fragrant.

Stir to mix all ingredients together.

Remove the tomatoes and garlic from the pan, add fresh chopped basil.

Place tomatoes on a platter and spoon avocado cream over the top.

Garnish with whole basil leaves.

# ELOTES – MEXICAN ROASTED CORN

This Mexican Corn, known as Elote, is smothered in mayonnaise and Parmesan. You add a little, smoky chili powder or smoked paprika and then immediately dive in. The corn is grilled, which makes it pop with juicy, sweetness.

ERVINGS: 4

**INGREDIENTS:**

4 ears of corn

¼ cup melted butter

½ cup mayonnaise

2 cups Parmesan cheese

2 teaspoons chili powder

4 limes, quartered

**METHOD:**

Soak corn in water for at least one hour

Heat the grill.

Grill corn in husk over high heat until husk is charred and corn is cooked, about 20 minutes.

Remove from grill, then pull back husk and husk completely along with any remaining silk.

Spread a bit of mayonnaise over each ear of corn.

Sprinkle the Parmesan cheese generously on the corn, making sure it covers all sides.

Sprinkle chili powder evenly across the corn.

Serve immediately with fresh limes to squeeze over the top of each.

# SKILLET POTATOES

This skillet potato recipe is adapted from a recipe I learned to make from my grandmother. She often served these crispy potatoes with a meatloaf dinner or when they would have the whole family over for brunch. Bacon drippings are the key ingredient in these crispy skillet potatoes and we often throw this together to accompany steaks with sautéed mushrooms and a nice red wine for a hearty dinner.

SERVINGS: 4

**INGREDIENTS:**

1 pound Russet potatoes, unpeeled, cut in 1/2 inch cubes

2 tablespoons bacon drippings

2 tablespoons butter

salt and pepper

**METHOD:**

Heat the bacon drippings and butter in a large skillet over medium high heat until the butter is bubbling.

Add the potatoes and season with salt and pepper.

Cook, stirring occasionally until the potatoes are browned on all sides.

Turn the heat to low and continue cooking until the potatoes are cooked through.

Serve immediately.

# POLENTA

Polenta is one of those flexible and versatile dishes that can be prepared in advance, then when needed it can be cut into small pieces to grill or pan fry and serve as a substantial side dish. It can also be flavored and garnished with Parmesan cheese, butter or a combination of spices.

SERVINGS: 4-6

**INGREDIENTS:**

4 cups water

1 cup coarse polenta (also known as corn grits)

salt

2 tablespoons butter

**METHOD:**

In a sauce pan, bring water to a boil over high heat.

When the water boils, reduce heat to medium and whisk in the polenta.

Reduce heat to low and cook for about 45 minutes, stirring often.

Add more water if needed to keep a creamy consistency.

Remove from heat and stir in butter and salt as needed.

Serve warm with meal or reserve by pouring the mixture onto a small cookie sheet and refrigerate.

To grill or pan fry, cut into small pieces and brush both sides with oil. Grill or fry for about three minutes per side until heated through.

# DESSERTS

Admittedly, we do not serve dessert on the boat for our guests very often. In fact, the first time I actually did create a dessert on board was for a progressive dock party. Ever since that time, all we have really offered as a dessert has been some variation on grilled fruit with ice cream or skewered melon and berries with different sauces. Here is our humble dessert section. Hope you enjoy and find some inspiration from this.

# GRILLED PINEAPPLE SATAY

We enjoy grilled pineapple. This recipe combines the fruit's natural sweetness with the tart and spicy flavors of lime and chili powder. It is a very simple dessert to serve to a group with very little effort yet seems to leave a lasting impression.

SERVINGS: 4-6

**INGREDIENTS:**

1 fresh pineapple

2 tablespoons brown sugar

1 lime, juiced

1 tablespoon olive oil

1 tablespoon honey or agave nectar

1 tablespoon chili powder

salt

**METHOD:**

Peel pineapple.

Cut lengthwise into six wedges, then remove core.

In a small bowl, mix remaining ingredients until blended.

Brush pineapple with the glaze.

Grill pineapple over medium heat for about four minutes per side.

After pineapple has been grilled, skewer and serve.

# MELON AND BERRY KABOBS WITH CHOCOLATE BALSAMIC

People are often impressed by the beautiful presentation when we serve these, yet it is really just a result of the ripe colorful melon and berries used to create these melon and berry kabobs. Try the recipe here or create your own with other variations of fresh fruit.

SERVINGS: 4-6

**KABOBS**

**INGREDIENTS:**

1 small, seedless watermelon, cleaned and diced in one-inch cubes

1 cantaloupe, cleaned and diced in one-inch cubes

1 quart strawberries, cleaned and hulled

1 pint blackberries

**METHOD:**

Using metal skewers, place melon and berries on skewers in a similar fashion for each.

**CHOCOLATE BALSAMIC**

**INGREDIENTS:**

4 cups balsamic vinegar

2 cups water

1 cup sugar

1 cup unsweetened cocoa powder

1/2 teaspoon kosher salt

2 teaspoons pure vanilla

**METHOD:**

Pour balsamic vinegar in a pan and cook over high heat until reduced by half.

In another sauce pan, bring the sugar, salt and water to a boil, add the cocoa powder and stir until slightly thickened.

Remove from heat and add the vanilla.

Mix the two cups reduced vinegar and two cups syrup together, then let cool.

Serve kabobs on a platter and drizzle sauce over all the kabobs.

# ICE CREAM WITH APPLE BRANDY SAUCE

This recipe goes back to my early years as a cook. As with many others, the original source has been lost with the passage of time. The apples simmer slowly in butter, then the juice of the apples lends itself to a rich buttery caramel sauce with the addition of brown sugar and apple brandy. This is best served warm over vanilla ice cream.

SERVINGS: 4

**INGREDIENTS:**

2 tablespoons butter

4 pink lady apples, finely sliced

1 cinnamon stick

1 teaspoon ground cinnamon

4 tbsp brown sugar

juice of ½ lemon

4 tablespoons apple brandy

vanilla ice cream

**METHOD:**

Place butter in a large skillet and melt over low heat.

Add apples, cinnamon stick, cinnamon and cook over medium heat, stirring constantly until apples are golden and slightly tender, about five minutes.

Add brown sugar, lemon juice and brandy and cook for another five minutes until liquid begins to turn brown and caramelize.

If heat is too high, the alcohol from the brandy may flame a little. If this happens, place a lid over the skillet until it burns out.

Remove from heat.

Scoop one large scoop of ice cream into each of four coupe or martini glasses.

Top with apple brandy sauce and garnish with fresh mint.

WITHDRAWN